A Hands-On, Minds-On Approach

Grades 2-3

Written by
Elizabeth Flikkema

Cover Design by
Matthew Van Zomeren

Inside Art by
Peggy Falk

Published by Instructional Fair • TS Denison
an imprint of

About the Book

The Inquiry Science series was designed and tested by classroom teachers familiar with the *National Science Education Standards*. It is the goal of the series to apply the standards in a user-friendly format.

Promote minds-on learning by challenging students to verbalize their observations and make inferences. Ask simple questions such as the following: What just happened? Why do you think that happened? What did you discover? Where have you seen that before? You may raise students' awareness and highlight the importance of the science process skills through discussion.

Credits

Author: Elizabeth Flikkema
Cover Design: Matthew Van Zomeren
Inside Illustrations: Peggy Falk
Project Director/Editor: Elizabeth Flikkema
Editors: Wendy Roh Jenks,
  Sharon Kirkwood
Page Design: Pat Geasler

About The Author

Elizabeth Flikkema taught second grade for eight years in Holland, Michigan. She earned a bachelor's degree in English along with her teaching certificate. Ms. Flikkema conducted graduate work at Western Michigan University. While teaching, Ms. Flikkema was very involved with curriculum development for all subjects, but her favorite work was for the science curriculum committee where she developed her love of teaching science through inquiry.

McGraw-Hill Children's Publishing

A Division of The McGraw-Hill Companies

Published by Instructional Fair • TS Denison
An imprint of McGraw-Hill Children's Publishing
Copyright © 2000 McGraw-Hill Children's Publishing

Limited Reproduction Permission: Permission to duplicate these materials is limited to the person for whom they are purchased. Reproduction for an entire school or school district is unlawful and strictly prohibited.

Send all inquiries to:
McGraw-Hill Children's Publishing
3195 Wilson Drive NW
Grand Rapids, Michigan 49544

All Rights Reserved • Printed in the United States of America

Simple Machines—grades 2-3
ISBN: 1-56822-947-X

Table of Contents

Movement
  Push and Pull
    Analyze the motions involved in a demonstration 4–5

Inclined Plane/Ramp
  Rolling Down the Ramp
    Explore how shape, weight, and material alter the effects of gravity 6–7
  Raise the Ramp
    Raise and lower the ramp to change the movement of cars 8–9
  Carry a Heavy Load
    Discover the effect of weight on speed of an object in motion 10–11
  Rough Road
    Explore how friction affects an object in motion 12–13

Wedge
  Wedges
    Classify objects containing wedges by the job they perform 14–15

Wheel and Axle
  Rollers
    Explore properties of a wheel 16–17
  Can You Make It Roll?
    Discover the importance of an axle 18–19

Lever
  Your Lever Best
    Explore how a lever makes work easier 20–21
  Teeter-Totter
    Balance a lever by moving the load 22–23

Pulley
  A Pull for a Pulley
    Explore how a pulley makes work easier 24–25

Screw
  Round and Round
    Compare a screw to an inclined plane 26–27

Complex Machines
  Complex Machines
    Discover simple machines within complex machines 28–29
  Making Work Easier
    Compare work with and without machines 30–31

Performance-Based Assessment
    A rubric of student performance . . . 32

Push and Pull

Gearing Up
Brainstorm a list of things in the classroom or around the school that move or have moving parts. When you have a good list, ask students to try to name what is causing the movement in each case. Hang the list in the classroom for later reference. (See "Complex Machines" on page 28.) When the students have more information, they will sort the list into categories according to the type of simple machine that is involved.

:::
Process Skills Used
- observing
- inferring
- forming a hypothesis
- communicating
:::

Guided Discovery
Background for the teacher:
One of the basic concepts involved in the study of simple machines is movement. Every movement is caused by either a push or a pull. Sometimes the pull is gravity.

Materials for demonstration:
table
straw broom with a long handle
aluminum pie tin
plastic cup (with weight inside)
two thick sponges
ball of string (must fit in cup)

Directions for the activity:
Place the cup near the edge of the table. Place the pie tin on top of the cup so the edge of the tin extends over the edge of the table. Place two sponges on the pie tin over the cup. Place the ball of string on top. (The cup, sponges, and ball of string are all aligned vertically.)

Standing in front of the setup, step on the broom bristles and pull the broom handle toward you. When you release the broom handle, it will strike the pie tin. The pie tin and sponges will be pushed forward and the string will fall into the cup.

Responding to Discovery
Discussion starters:
- Which items moved in this demonstration?
- Which items moved because they were pushed?
- Which items moved because they were pulled?
- Is every movement caused by either a push or a pull?

Applications and Extensions
Allow students to play outside with balls, jump ropes, and other playground equipment. Ask them to analyze and classify their movements as pushes or pulls. It is early to introduce the term gravity, but you may lead them to discover that when something falls to the ground without a push, it is being pulled.

:::
Real-World Applications
- What objects in the kitchen have moving parts?
:::

© Instructional Fair • TS Denison

IF20854 *Simple Machines*

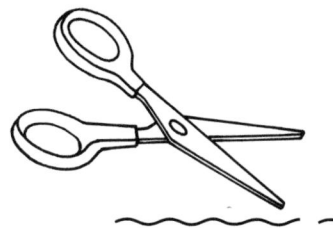

Name _____

Push and Pull

Draw the broom demonstration.

Draw the setup.

Draw the materials after the broom hits the Frisbee.

What items moved in this demonstration?
_____
_____

Which items were pushed, and which were pulled?
_____
_____

What object would you like to change in this demonstration? Why?
_____
_____

Try your change and describe the results.
_____
_____

© Instructional Fair • TS Denison

IF20854 *Simple Machines*

Rolling Down the Ramp

Gearing Up

Use a ramp and ramp stand set at a middle setting. Hold up a tennis ball and ask students to predict what will happen when you release the ball at the top of the ramp. Acknowledge predictions and release the ball. Discuss what happened and ask students to propose explanations.

Process Skills Used
- making a model
- predicting
- recording data
- proposing explanations

Guided Discovery

Background for the teacher:

Simple machines create forces that cause movement. The first simple machine the class will explore is the inclined plane, or ramp. This discovery explores how shape, weight, and material alter the effects of gravity. Do not change the ramp height in this discovery.

Materials needed for each group:

ramp and ramp stand
potato   block   toy car
ball   sponge   stone
eraser   ruler
wad of paper
other small objects

Directions for the activity:

Direct each group to set up a ramp. (A ramp may be made with a narrow sheet of masonite or thin wood leaned against a 6-inch stack of books.)

Students will make their predictions then test the behavior of each object on the ramp. Students should always start the objects at the same point on the ramp. You may wish to discuss ahead of time what "rolling a little" means and what it means to "roll far." Each student should record the actual behavior of the objects by drawing the objects in the correct section of the chart on page 7.

Responding to Discovery

Discuss what is making the objects move. Why do some objects move more than others? Why do some objects move without rolling? How does a ramp cause things to move?

Applications and Extensions

Use the playground slide as a ramp and observe how different and larger objects behave on a ramp.

Real-World Applications
- What causes an avalanche?
- Do different body positions on the slide make students move easier?

© Instructional Fair • TS Denison
IF20854 Simple Machines

Name _____

Rolling Down the Ramp

Make a prediction. What do you think each object will do on the ramp? Draw each object in the chart to record your predictions.

Roll a little	Roll far	Doesn't roll

What did each object do on the ramp? Draw each object in the chart to record the actual movement.

Rolled a little	Rolled far	Didn't roll

Raise the Ramp

Gearing Up

Set up a demonstration ramp and ask students to predict what will happen when you place a toy car on the ramp. Demonstrate and ask students to describe how far the car moved. Ask students to propose methods for measuring the distance that the car traveled from the bottom of the ramp. Come to a concensus so all students use the same measurement system (standard or nonstandard units).

> *Process Skills Used*
> - measuring
> - comparing
> - recording data

Guided Discovery

Background for the teacher:

Students will discover that as the ramp height increases, the cars will travel farther.

Materials needed for each group:

ramp and ramp stand
measurement tools
toy car
(Buy the same style for each group. Cheap models fall apart quickly.)

Directions for the activity:

Inspire curiosity by saying, "I wonder what will happen if I change the incline (increase their vocabulary) of the ramp?" Students will work in groups to explore how a higher or lower ramp changes the distance the car travels. Allow students to explore and record several trials.

Responding to Discovery

As students are working, circulate among the groups and ask questions that challenge students to think about what they are doing. Encourage them to try other variations. "What did you find out?" "I wonder what would happen if . . ."

Applications and Extensions

Have students make a class graph showing how far the cars traveled at each ramp height. They may have to calculate an average or look for common distances. Write a class hypothesis statement on the graph. For example, "When the ramp is higher, the car travels farther." Hang the graph and the hypothesis in the hall along with student drawings of the activity.

> *Real-World Applications*
> - Roller coaster rides
> - Coasting down a steep slope on a bicycle

© Instructional Fair • TS Denison

IF20854 *Simple Machines*

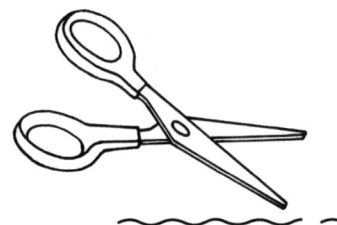

Raise the Ramp

Name _____

Record the distance the car travels on each trial.

High Ramp   **Trials**
                       1. _____
                       2. _____
                       3. _____

Medium Ramp   **Trials**
                       1. _____
                       2. _____
                       3. _____

Low Ramp   **Trials**
                       1. _____
                       2. _____
                       3. _____

How did you measure the distance the car traveled?
_____

What did you find out?
_____
_____

Why do you think that happened?
_____
_____

Do you think other groups found out the same thing? Explain.
_____
_____

© Instructional Fair • TS Denison   IF20854 *Simple Machines*

Carry a Heavy Load

Gearing Up

Set up a longer, wider ramp to fit a large toy truck. (If you do not have a truck, ask a student to bring in a truck from home.) Ask students to predict what the truck will do on the ramp. Release the truck at the top of the ramp and discuss what happens. Repeat and measure speed and distance traveled. If several students bring in large trucks, hold a contest to see which truck is fastest, travels farthest, or moves the smoothest.

Process Skills Used
- measuring
- comparing
- communicating

Guided Discovery

Background for the teacher:

Students will discover that a heavy load causes the truck to move faster and travel farther from the end of the ramp. Forces can change the speed or direction of objects in motion.

Materials for demonstration:

36" x 12" ramp
ramp stand (Lean the ramp against a chair.)
measurement tools

Directions for the activity:

Ask the students to make predictions about what will happen when you load the truck with heavy books or bricks. Release the truck at the top of the ramp and have students make observations. Repeat the activity with and without the load until students can make hypotheses. Then ask, "How can we prove that our hypothesis is always true?" Try out some of the students' suggestions.

Responding to Discovery

Have students draw pictures of the truck on the ramp with and without the load. They should describe the action of the truck.

Applications and Extensions

Explore how heavy and light people move differently on the playground slide. Have students explore ways to make themselves move faster or slower on the slide.

Real-World Applications
- Why must truck drivers be very careful with heavy loads?

© Instructional Fair • TS Denison IF20854 *Simple Machines*

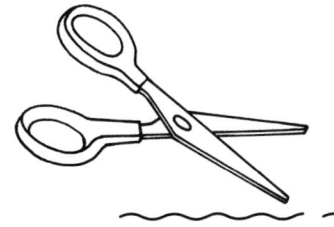

Name _____

Carry a Heavy Load

I predict that the truck with a heavy load will _____
_____
_____

Draw a picture of the truck and the ramp.

Without the load	**With the load**

Were you surprised by what you observed? Explain.
_____
_____

What caused the truck to move? _____
_____

Hypothesis _____
_____
_____

© Instructional Fair • TS Denison   11   IF20854 Simple Machines

Rough Road

Gearing Up

Ask students if they have ever been in a car on an icy road. Discuss what the texture of the road was like. Discuss whether the car acts differently on icy roads and gravel roads. Tell the students that today they will explore how the texture of the ramp affects the distance a car travels.

Process Skills Used
- measuring
- comparing
- communicating

Guided Discovery

Background for the teacher:

Friction is a force that causes a change in motion.

Materials needed for each group:

three grades of sandpaper
three ramps
three ramp stands
a toy car

Directions for the activity:

Tape a strip of sandpaper down the length of each ramp—one type of sandpaper per ramp. Label the ramps with Post-it Notes: Fine, Medium, and Coarse. Set each ramp at the same height. Students should predict what the car will do on the ramp before releasing the car from the same spot on each ramp. Measure and record the distance the car travels.

Responding to Discovery

Using only the collected data, students write hypotheses about the texture of the ramp and the movement of the car. Have them draw the details of their explorations.

Applications and Extensions

Apply other surfaces to the ramp, such as aluminum foil, waxed paper, and construction paper. Discuss how the textures affect the distance the car travels.

Real-World Applications
- Discuss the experience of rollerskating or biking on rough roads.

© Instructional Fair • TS Denison   IF20854 *Simple Machines*

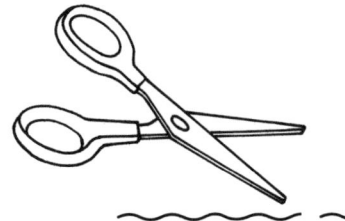

Name _____

Rough Road

Record your prediction and the actual distance traveled by the toy car on each type of sandpaper.

Sandpaper	Prediction	Trial 1	Trial 2	Trial 3
Fine				
Medium				
Coarse				

Circle which type of sandpaper caused the car to travel the shortest distance.   **fine   medium   coarse**

Hypothesis _____
_____

Were you surprised by your observations? Explain.
_____
_____

Where have you seen something like this in real life?
Draw a picture to explain.

© Instructional Fair • TS Denison   IF20854 Simple Machines

Wedges

Gearing Up

If you have an opportunity to take a field trip to a simulation of log cabin living, it is an ideal location to see wedges in action (farming and wood-cutting tools).

Give each student a carrot stick. Tell students that a wedge is a simple machine that uses force to come between two things or to split something. Ask students to use a wedge found on their bodies to split the carrot stick into two pieces.

> *Process Skills Used*
> - observing
> - classifying

Guided Discovery

Background for the teacher:

The second simple machine the class will explore is the wedge. A wedge uses force to come between two things. It may tighten (door stop), hold (nail, staple), or split (ax). An ax is a wedge used to split wood. A plow is a wedge that splits the soil. A saw and other cutting tools contain wedges.

Materials needed for each group:

a variety of objects (or pictures) containing a wedge:

cookie cutter   nail   knife
cheese grater   staple   plow
potato peeler   tack   door wedge
nail clipper   scissors   zipper
can opener (one for punching holes and another for removing the top)

Directions for the activity:

Give each group a box of items. Students should observe each object and identify where the wedges are located. The wedge is often shaped like a triangle, coming to a sharp point.

First, the group should discuss and classify each object into one of the three jobs (tighten, hold, split). Then students should draw each object in their charts and draw an arrow pointing to the wedge on the object.

Responding to Discovery

Bring the groups together and assign each member of the group a number. Hold up one of the objects from the box. Call a number so one member of each group is selected. Ask each of the selected students one question about the object. (Where is the wedge on this object? What is its job (hold, tighten, or split)? When is it used? Repeat with the other objects.

Applications and Extensions

Make sugar cookies. As students use cookie cutters, they can observe how the sharp edge "splits" the dough.

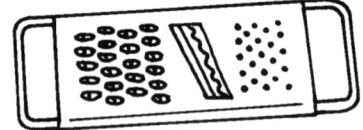

> *Real-World Applications*
> - Discuss the work of wedges found on complex machines in real life, such as on a snowplow.

© Instructional Fair • TS Denison

IF20854 *Simple Machines*

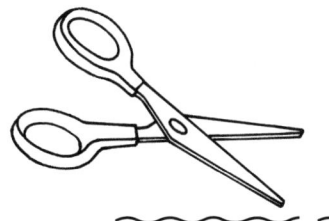

Name _____

Wedges

Draw each object in the correct "job" category. Draw an arrow to show where the wedge is located.

These wedges **tighten**.

These wedges **hold**.

These wedges **split**.

© Instructional Fair • TS Denison   IF20854 *Simple Machines*

Rollers

Gearing Up

Brainstorm with the class a list of words that are related to rolling or turning (spin, round, rotate). Ask the students to use those words in a poem about wheels.

Process Skills Used
- observing
- inferring
- communicating

Guided Discovery

Background for the teacher:

The third simple machine the class will explore is the wheel and axle. You want students to gain experience with the properties that cause wheels to roll. Rounded objects roll while objects with flat sides slide.

Materials needed for each group:
a variety of rolling and nonrolling objects (blocks, apple, potato, sponge, can, ruler, key, etc.)

Directions for the activity:
Challenge students to sort the given objects into two categories: *objects that roll* and *objects that slide*. Ask students to predict whether or not the object will roll before they attempt to roll it.

Responding to Discovery

Students should observe the objects that did roll and describe the characteristics they have in common. They should also write what the nonrolling objects have in common. Ask them to write hypotheses about what characteristics allow objects to roll. They can test their hypotheses on other objects.

Applications and Extensions

Pose the following question for students to respond to: "If we were going to make a car out of a shoe box, what objects might make good wheels?"

Real-World Applications
- Explore spin toys.
- How do ball bearings help things move?

© Instructional Fair • TS Denison

IF20854 *Simple Machines*

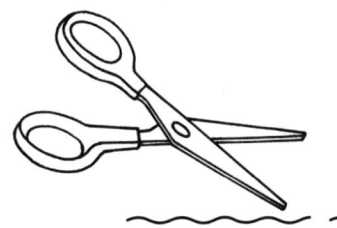

Name _____

Rollers

Write the name of the object in the first column. Write a "yes" or "no" in the other columns to indicate whether or not the object can roll or slide.

Object	Rolls	Slides

On lined paper, describe the properties that make an object roll.

Can You Make It Roll?

Gearing Up

Give each group of students a block of wood and ask them if they can make it roll. Most students will see that they cannot. Then offer them other materials, such as pencils, straws, erasers, small paper plates, spools, and tape. Listen to their ideas about how they might use the materials. Then for the discovery lesson, allow them to experiment with their proposals.

Process Skills Used
- observing
- predicting
- making a model
- communicating

Guided Discovery

Background for the teacher:

Adding rollers under a vehicle will reduce friction and allow it to move, but the rollers do not stay with the vehicle. A wheel on its own will not make an object roll—an axle is needed. The axle is affixed to the vehicle and the wheels spin on the axle.

Materials needed for each group:

paper plates   pencils   spools
block of wood   straws   tape
pencil-top erasers (for wheel caps)
Allow students to propose other materials.

Directions for the activity:

Students may wish to observe the mechanics of a wagon or other wheeled vehicle. They will quickly see the need for an axle when they try to tape a spool or paper plate directly to the wood block.

Some students may just put the block on the straws or pencils and let the block glide over the straws or pencils. They will notice that the block of wood eventually rolls off the rollers. This is an example of how ball bearings are used in machinery to allow parts to move with little friction.

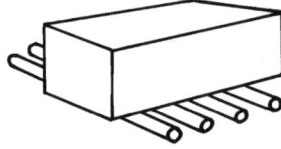

Responding to Discovery

Have students draw pictures of their vehicles on the activity sheet. Have them label the wheels and axles.

Applications and Extensions

Brainstorm a list of things that move on wheels. In each instance, list what pushes the wheeled vehicle. For example, a skateboard is pushed by a kick.

Real-World Applications
- Observe pictures of a wheel and axle on a car or other large vehicle.
- Study the wheels and axles on a bicycle.

© Instructional Fair • TS Denison   IF20854 Simple Machines

Name _____

Can You Make It Roll?

Draw the plan for your vehicle.

Draw the finished vehicle.

Your Lever Best

Gearing Up

Use a ruler as a lever and catapult a marshmallow into the classroom. When the excitement dies down, ask the class to describe all the movements involved in that action. Ask the following questions: Where was the push? Where was the pull? What was the effect? How can a lever make things move easily?

Process Skills Used
- observing
- comparing
- making a model

Guided Discovery

Background for the teacher:

The fourth simple machine the class will explore is the lever. A lever is an inclined plane, or ramp, with the fulcrum (ramp stand) in a different location. A lever can make work easier—it can help you lift a heavy object or add force to a movement. To give the lever the best advantage, place the fulcrum close to the load and use a long lever.

Materials needed for each group:

large, heavy box
6' length of 2" x 4" wood
2' length of 2" x 4" wood
Use a chunk of wood for a fulcrum.

Directions for the activity:

Challenge students to lift a heavy box without any simple machines. Then, give them the levers and fulcrum.

Encourage students to explore the easiest way to lift the box. Lead them to discover that a short lever is not as effective as a long lever. A fulcrum close to the load is also more effective. Have students repeat the experiment to be sure that the lever they created is the best design.

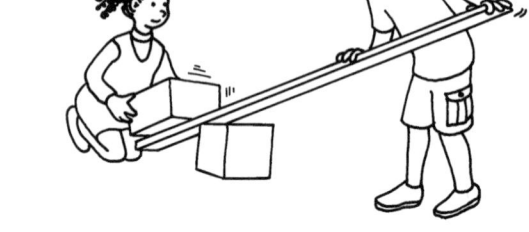

Responding to Discovery

Have students draw (on page 21) the lever that worked best to lift the load. They should label each part.

Applications and Extensions

Propose a challenge: Can students design a lever that will allow one student to lift the teacher?

Real-World Applications
- Look at everyday objects that contain levers. Discuss how the lever on each machine makes work easier.

hammer	scissors
pliers	wheelbarrow
nutcracker	nail clipper
nail extracter	broom
shovel	stapler

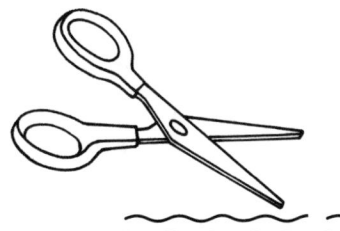

Name _____

Your Lever Best

A lever can make lifting easier. Try each of these levers to lift a heavy object. Move the fulcrum closer to, and farther from, the load.

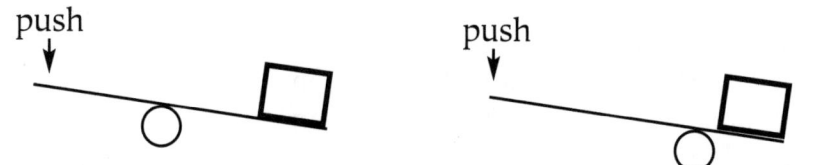 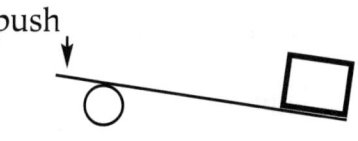

Draw the lever that worked best for you.
Label the fulcrum, push (force), and load.

List tools and machines that use a lever.

_____
_____
_____
_____

Teeter-Totter

Gearing Up

Make a classroom teeter-totter with a 6-foot-long 2" x 4" piece of lumber. Use a sturdy student chair as the fulcrum. Experiment with putting different-sized students on opposite ends of the teeter-totter. Soon they will discover that moving backward and forward on the board will help balance the weight. Repeat several times and discuss what the students discovered. **Note:** Keep safety in mind as you explore this simple teeter-totter. An adult should make sure that the board does not fall off the fulcrum.

Process Skills Used
- observing
- measuring
- making a model
- inferring

Guided Discovery

Background for the teacher:

A teeter-totter is a form of lever with the fulcrum in the center. In this lesson, students can explore how the position of the load can make lifting a heavy item easier. Students can balance uneven masses by moving the masses up and down the lever. Moving the masses away from the center produces more force.

Materials for each group or student:

one ruler
one pencil
two books of equal thickness
seven pennies or linking cubes

Directions for the activity:

Students tape the pencil across the center of the ruler. Then, they place the pencil and ruler between the two books. Have them place a penny at each end of the ruler and adjust until the ruler is balanced. On the activity sheet, students draw the location of the pennies on the ruler. As they stack another penny on top of one of the pennies, they can discuss what happens.

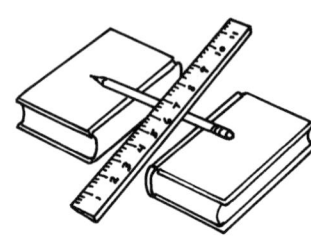

Have students explore how they must adjust the penny to balance with the stack. They draw the position of the pennies on the activity sheet. Students repeat this by adding pennies one by one to one side and balancing with one penny on the other.

Responding to Discovery

Discuss student observations and relate to something they have seen before (for example, balancing on a boat, bench, or teeter-totter).

Applications and Extensions

Have students explore how a balance scale compares the relative weights of two objects. Use a balance scale with gram masses.

Real-World Applications
- Balancing in a canoe or other boat

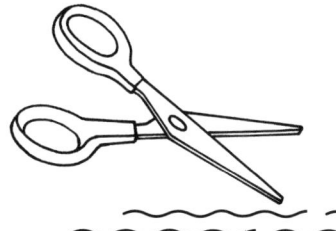

Name _____
Teeter-Totter

Balance one penny with a stack of pennies by moving the single penny up and down the ruler. Draw the pennies' locations in each trial.

Balance one penny with . . .

one penny.   two pennies.

_____○_____   _____○_____

three pennies.   four pennies.

_____○_____   _____○_____

five pennies.   six pennies.

_____○_____   _____○_____

What did you find out about balancing on a teeter-totter?
_____
_____
_____

Would this work every time? _____

Explain. _____
_____

© Instructional Fair • TS Denison   IF20854 *Simple Machines*

A Pull for a Pulley

Gearing Up

Ask students how the flag can move **up** the flag pole when the flag raiser is pulling **down** on the rope. Listen for explanations. Allow students to observe a pulley and turn the wheel inside.

Process Skills Used
- observing
- communicating
- making a model

Guided Discovery

Background for the teacher:

The fifth simple machine the class will explore is the pulley. A pulley is used to lift a heavy load vertically. It can also be used to raise an object higher than a person's reach. A pulley reverses the directon of the force. That is why you can use a downward force to lift an object up. The pulley reduces the amount of force needed to lift a heavy object.

Materials for each student:

an empty spool of thread
a wire hanger or other sturdy wire
wire cutter (for teacher use)
rope

Directions:

In advance, cut the bottom off the wire hangers. The students bend the two ends of the hanger so they go through the opposite ends of the spool. When the wires come out the opposite ends of the spool, they should bend the wires down. This prevents the spool from slipping out, but allows it to turn freely. Hook the top of the hanger on a solid spot, such as the back of a chair. Tie a rope to a heavy object. Have students first attempt to lift the heavy object by the rope. Then, they can thread the rope around the spool and use the spool as a pulley to lift the object. They should compare the amount of force needed to lift the object with and without the pulley.

Have two students work together to create a message-sending system between their desks. They can tie their ropes together in a loop around both of their spool pulleys. Then, they can affix a message or object to the rope and pull the message between them.

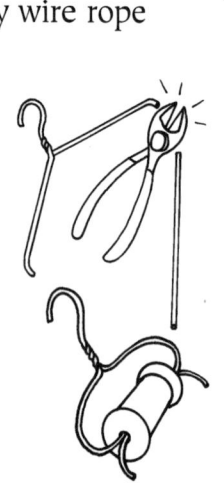

Responding to Discovery

Discuss how a pulley is different from a wheel and axle.

Applications and Extensions

Ask students to propose and design a pulley system that sends messages to the office from the classroom (or another point if this is not practical). It may require more than two pulleys.

Use a purchased moveable pulley to demonstrate how a pulley can be used to lift a load.

Real-World Applications
- Study the pulley system on mini-blinds on a window at home.

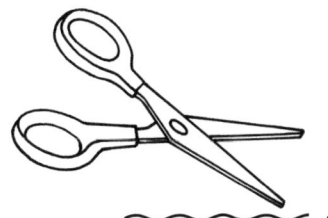

Name _____

A Pull for a Pulley

In the flagpole drawing, draw arrows to show the direction of the moving rope, pulley, and flag.

Draw yourself lifting the heavy object with a rope. Then draw yourself lifting the object with the help of your pulley. Draw arrows to show the direction of movements.

Lifting without the pulley

Lifting with the pulley

© Instructional Fair • TS Denison

25

IF20854 *Simple Machines*

Round and Round

Gearing up

Pass out a variety of screws for students to observe and explore. Ask students to place a fingernail in the threads at the tip of the screw and turn the screw with the other hand. Ask students to describe what happens. They should notice how the finger moves up the screw as it is turned. The finger moves down when the screw is turned in the opposite direction.

Process Skills Used
- observing
- communicating

Guided Discovery

Background for the teacher:

The sixth simple machine the class will explore is the screw. A screw, like a nail, is a fastener. It can hold two things together. Screws can be found in pencil sharpeners, corkscrews, drills, vices, bit and braces, as well as a corkscrew slide on the playground.

Materials needed for each student:

Activity I:
screwdriver and a variety of screws (Choose screws with different widths between the threads.)
soft wood or wood with drill holes for students to screw into

Activity II:
plain paper   scissors
marker   pencil

Directions for Activity I

Have students examine the threads on a variety of screws. They should pay particular attention to the distance between the threads. Have them predict which screw will be easiest to screw into the wood. Have them carefully use the screwdriver to try each screw and record their observations. *Safety note: students should wear safety goggles while using tools.*

Directions for Activity II:

Students learn that a screw is like an inclined plane (ramp) wrapped around a cylinder. Have students cut a triangle from a sheet of paper by cutting diagonally from corner to corner. Students should trace the diagonal edge of the triangle with a marker. Ask students to identify which simple machine the triangle resembles (inclined plane). Then, beginning with the short end, students wrap the triangle around a pencil. Compare the wrapped pencil to a screw. Ask students to compare the screw to an inclined plane.

Responding to Discovery

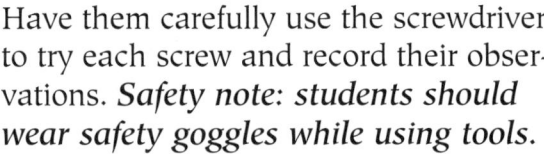

Students complete the activity sheet. Did all students get the same results? Discuss why certain screws might be easier to screw into wood. Discuss why some screws are sold as wood screws and some as metal screws. Discuss how a screw is like a ramp.

Applications and Extensions

Explore tools and machines that contain screws (see background).

Real-World Applications
- Study fasteners such as nuts and bolts, nails, staples, and screws.
- Research Archimedes' screw.

© Instructional Fair • TS Denison   IF20854 *Simple Machines*

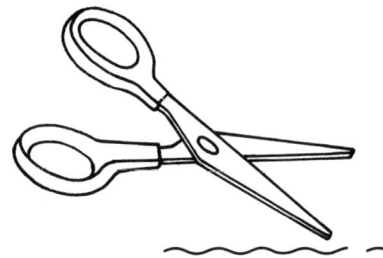

Name _____

Round and Round

Draw four different screws. Pay close attention to the width of the threads.

Which screw do you think will be easiest to screw into the wood? _____ Why do you think that? _____
_____

Use a screwdriver to screw each one into a block of wood. Draw the screws in order from easiest to hardest to screw into wood.

Easiest   **Hardest**

Explain your observations. _____
_____
_____

© Instructional Fair • TS Denison   IF20854 *Simple Machines*

Complex Machines

Gearing Up

Take the cover off the classroom pencil sharpener and allow students to analyze what simple machines they see.

Explain that simple machines are the elements that make up larger, or more complex, machines. Machines make work easier.

Process Skills Used
- observing
- comparing
- classifying

Guided Discovery

Background for the teacher:

When two or more simple machines are combined, they become a complex machine.

Materials for each student:

chart on page 29
objects found around home, classroom, garage, etc.

Directions for the activity:

Ask students to look around the classroom for any objects or tools that help them do work. They should list the objects in the chart and analyze the objects for what simple machines they contain. Have students take their charts home to add kitchen and garage tools and machines.

Responding to Discovery

Students bring their completed charts back to the classroom to compare. create a large wall chart and ask students to share the information they gathered. Discuss the variety of simple machines. Which simple machines seem to turn up most often? Were students surprised by what they found?

Refer to the chart created on the first day (page 4). This is a list of objects that move or have moving parts. This list would be a terrific starting point for completing the chart.

Applications and Extensions

If possible, visit a local machine factory. Ask students to look for the simple machines that make up the large, complex machines. Discuss the importance of simple machines in everything that moves.

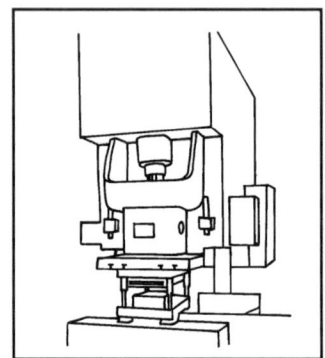

Real-World Applications
- Students can observe many simple machines in a car engine or in a carpenter's workshop. This should be done only with parental guidance.

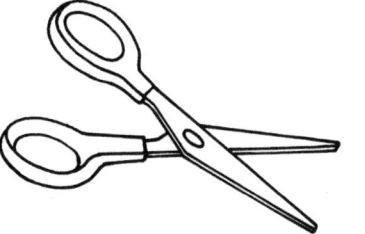

Name _____

Complex Machines

Look around the classroom, your kitchen, and your garage for complex machines. List the complex machines and make a check (✓) under each simple machine found in the complex machine. For example, a wheelbarrow contains a lever and a wheel and axle.

Simple Machines in Complex Machines

Object	Inclined plane	Wheel and axle	Screw	Pulley	Wedge	Lever
wheelbarrow		✓				✓

Making Work Easier

Gearing Up

Machines are meant to make work easier. Ask students how we can prove that work is easier with a given machine. Have one student beat an egg with a fork while another student uses an eggbeater. Who can make the eggs frothy faster? Ask students to predict and explain why before you begin. After the demonstration, discuss whether the eggbeater made work easier.

Process Skills Used
- observing
- comparing
- inferring

Guided Discovery

Background for the teacher:

A machine may be as simple as a shovel, which is made up of a wedge and a lever, but it makes work much easier. Imagine digging by hand or with a wedge alone.

Directions for the activity:

Ask students to think about how machines make work easier. They can complete the chart with the machines listed, then add other machines that they use or see in use.

Responding to Discovery

Students complete page 31. Discuss their observations. You may wish to have students work in groups to combine the information they gathered onto a poster that explains how machines can make work easier.

Applications and Extensions

Do some research to find out how some of these machines were first invented.

Design an invention that will make some types of work easier.

Real-World Applications
- Famous inventors
- Patents

© Instructional Fair • TS Denison 30 IF20854 *Simple Machines*

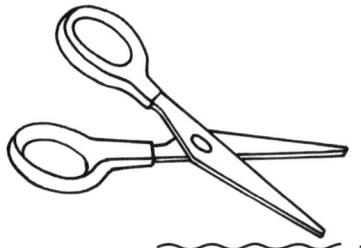

Name _____

Making Work Easier

Machine	What work does it do?	How could the work be done without it?
scissors		
can opener		
pencil sharpener		
shovel		
wheelbarrow		
cheese grater		
zipper		
stapler		
plow		
potato peeler		
bicycle		

© Instructional Fair • TS Denison   IF20854 *Simple Machines*

Performance-Based Assessment

3 = Exceeds expectations
2 = Consistently meets expectations
1 = Below expectations

Student Names

Lesson Investigation Discovery

Lesson 1:	Push and Pull
Lesson 2:	Rolling Down the Ramp
Lesson 3:	Raise the Ramp
Lesson 4:	Carry a Heavy Load
Lesson 5:	Rough Road
Lesson 6:	Wedges
Lesson 7:	Rollers
Lesson 8:	Can You Make It Roll?
Lesson 9:	Your Lever Best
Lesson 10:	Teeter-Totter
Lesson 11:	A Pull for a Pulley
Lesson 12:	Round and Round
Lesson 13:	Complex Machines
Lesson 14:	Making Work Easier

Specific Lesson Skills

- Can make reasonable hypothesis.
- Can measure with accuracy.
- Can make detailed observations.
- Can propose an explanation.
- Can follow directions.
- Displays curiosity.
- Works well within a small group or class.
- Participates in discussions.
- Can record data gathered from invstigations.
- Can classify data in meaningful categories.
- Can communicate through writing and/or drawing.
- Can apply what is learned to real-world situations.

© Instructional Fair • TS Denison

IF20854 *Simple Machines*